Prince William

W.O.W.*

✽ WILLIAM OF WALES

ELAINE LANDAU

A Gateway Biography
The Millbrook Press
Brookfield, Connecticut

For Sarah Sutin
—E.L.

Published by The Millbrook Press, Inc.
2 Old New Milford Road
Brookfield, CT 06804
www.millbrookpress.com

Cover photographs courtesy of © Alpha/Globe Photos, Inc.
Photographs courtesy of Globe Photos, Inc.: pp. 3 (© Steve Daniels/Alpha), 45
(© Alpha); Liaison Agency: pp. 7 (© F. Spooner), 13, 20 (top © Julian Parker;
bottom © Jayne Fincher), 25 (© Jayne Fincher), 30 (© Ian Jones/FSP), 34; ©
Corbis: pp. 8 (Bettmann), 41 (AFP); © Topham/The Image Works: pp. 10, 15,
16, 18, 23; AP/Wide World Photos: pp. 37, 43

Library of Congress Cataloging-in-Publication Data
Landau, Elaine.
Prince William : W.O.W., William of Wales / Elaine Landau.
p. cm. – (A Gateway biography)
On the t.p. an asterisk follows "W.O.W." followed by another asterisk and
"William of Wales."
Includes index.
Summary: A biography of the young prince, second in line to the British
throne, describing his background, interests, and how he has dealt with his
parents' divorce and his mother's tragic death.
ISBN 0-7613-2120-9 (lib. bdg.)
1. William, Prince, grandson of Elizabeth II, Queen of Great Britain, 1982—-
Juvenile literature. 2. Princes—Great Britain—Biography—Juvenile literature.
[1. William, Prince, grandson of Elizabeth II, Queen of Great Britain, 1982-
2. Princes.] I. Title. II. Series.
DA591.A45 W55548 2002 941.085'092—dc21 [B] 2001037070

CHAPTER ONE

A Present-Day Prince

PRINCE WILLIAM OF
WALES, IN
SEPTEMBER 2000

There have been many stories about handsome princes. Usually these are fairy tales. The young men in them have a lot in common. They are handsome, smart, and very charming. These young royals go on to become great kings. There's not a toad in the bunch.

That's how the storyline goes. But what about in real life? Are there really dashing young princes? Young men with dazzling smiles? Royals who could melt a young girl's heart?

Looking at Prince William of Britain, you might think so. Here is a prince who seems to have just stepped out of a storybook. This 6-foot-2 (nearly 2-meter) blond, blue-eyed royal is already a teen idol.

William is popular, rich, and famous. He is even an outstanding athlete and a good dancer. He has had many advantages. But this Prince Charming has not always led a charmed life.

At a fairly young age he had to deal with his parents' divorce and the scandal surrounding it. Later he would face the tragic death of his mother. It has been argued that William has already known more than his share of sorrow.

Yet remarkably he seems to have survived it with grace and dignity. Many believe a wonderful future awaits him. This is the story of Prince William. A present-day prince who will one day be king.

CHAPTER 2

A Royal Arrival

Prince William came into the world at 9:03 P.M. on June 21, 1982. Bells were rung throughout Britain. A new heir to the British throne was born. At that moment few things seemed more wonderful.

Prince William is the grandchild of Elizabeth II, the Queen of Britain. William's father is her son, Prince Charles of Wales. Less than a year earlier Charles had made Britain—and the world—happy with his marriage to a beautiful young British girl. Her name was Diana Frances Spencer.

Now the country adored their first child, Prince William Arthur Philip Louis. The 7-pound-10-ounce (3.5 kilogram) baby boy was the British monarchy's link with the future. His birth ensured that the royal line would continue.

Early on it was obvious that William's life would be different from those of past British kings. He was the first heir to the throne to be born in a hospital. In the past a delivery room, well staffed with doctors, nurses, and midwives, would have been set up in Buckingham Palace. But young William was born in St. Mary's Hospital in London. His wristband simply read "Baby Wales."

Some of the hospital staff were guests of honor at Prince William's christening. In a photo session following the ceremony, the young prince registered his first protest against being photographed. He cried loudly. His mother tried to calm him by allowing the baby to suck on her pinky finger.

William's great-grandmother, the queen mother, had turned eighty-two the day of the christening. She adored the new little prince. After hearing William cry, she noted that the future king of Britain had a fine set of lungs.

THE OFFICIAL PORTRAIT OF PRINCE WILLIAM AT HIS BAPTISM. SEATED FROM THE
LEFT ARE HIS GREAT-GRANDMOTHER ELIZABETH, PRINCE WILLIAM IN THE ARMS OF
HIS MOTHER, PRINCESS DIANA, AND QUEEN ELIZABETH II. BEHIND THEM ARE
PRINCE PHILIP, WILL'S GRANDFATHER, AND PRINCE CHARLES, HIS FATHER.

PRINCE WILLIAM TOOK HIS FIRST STEPS WHEN HE WAS NINE MONTHS OLD, DURING A TRIP WITH HIS PARENTS TO NEW ZEALAND AND AUSTRALIA.

Prince William's parents were quite involved in their son's daily care. This was a new idea for the royal family. Charles bathed his infant son and frequently changed his diapers as well. Prince William was Britain's first prince to wear disposable ones!

Diana spent even more time with the baby. She tried her best to always be there for William. When Prince William was just nine months old, his parents took him to New Zealand and Australia. During some of the trip the baby stayed with a nanny. His mother and father had important meetings to go to. But all their free time was spent with William.

William's father, Charles, had some definite ideas about choosing a nanny. He wanted his own former nanny, Mabel Anderson, for the job. She was well qualified and knew the ways of royalty.

But Diana refused to go along with this choice. She knew how she wanted her son raised. Princess Diana chose a forty-two-year-old woman named Barbara Barnes. Barnes was lighthearted and easy in her dealings with children. More important, Barnes acknowledged that Diana was in full charge.

It worked out well. Diana's duties sometimes took her away from William. Yet on the whole she was usually around to care for the prince. Whenever William was sick, Diana took over. She would move a cot into the nursery and sleep beside his crib.

Prince Charles's childhood had been very different. While growing up, his time with his parents

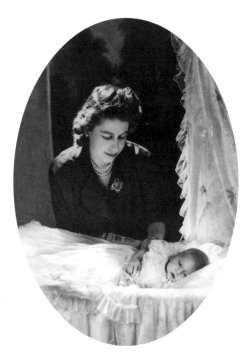

was quite limited. There were months at a time when he didn't see his mother at all. Often Queen Elizabeth II toured the British Commonwealth for extended periods. She also frequently vacationed without her children.

Diana was determined that William would know and love her. Her feelings were obvious. She was more interested in her son's happiness than in any royal duties.

CHAPTER 3

The Early Years

Prince William grew up with all of Britain watching. The beautiful royal baby soon turned into an active and very curious toddler. His mother called him "Wills." The prince's parents had other nicknames for him too. At one point they called him "Wombat"—which is a small Australian animal. When William was especially active, Diana referred to her son as the mini-tornado.

It took a lot of energy to keep up with toddler Will. He seemed to pull every cord, turn every knob, and push every bell. Once this led to trouble. In the summer of 1983 while at Balmoral Castle in

Scotland with his parents, William managed to push a special button in the nursery.

This set off a silent alarm alerting the local police. A big group of police officers rushed to the castle. They closed up the castle and began taking emergency measures. There was quite a bit of commotion until it was learned that Wills was the culprit.

William was hardly well behaved either at home or on vacation. He was known to scatter his toys wherever he went. In addition, this future king of Britain liked to flush various household items down the toilet. He even dropped in a pair of his father's shoes!

None of this seemed to upset his parents. For a time, the prince was treated as a royal child who could do no wrong. He was pampered instead of disciplined. But as the months passed, Charles and Diana began to rethink their parenting methods.

That was partly because William's place as an only child was about to end. His mother, Princess Diana, had become pregnant. On September 15, 1984, she gave birth to Prince Henry Charles Albert David. The boy was called "Harry," and he would be William's only sibling. The press described the royal brothers as "the heir and the spare."

WILL AND HIS NEW BABY BROTHER, HARRY

William took to Harry almost immediately. He always wanted to cuddle and play with the baby. At Harry's christening, William wanted to hold his little brother during the ceremony. When told that he couldn't, he was not happy. Will began running around the room.

Despite his young age, it was expected that the prince would behave at this official gathering. His grandmother, the queen, even told him to quiet down. But he refused to listen to her or anyone else. To make matters worse, several television crews were there. That meant that the nation would learn about the incident.

Before long, the situation worsened. During a visit to Birkhall, the queen's home in Scotland, William ran recklessly through the dining room. He knocked things over and created quite a mess. He was also disrespectful to the servants there. During the young prince's stay, the staff had begun to speak poorly of him.

By now, even Diana admitted there was a problem. William had become demanding at home too. He insisted that others put away his toys for him. He refused to go to bed when told. Many felt that William was turning his mother into a servant.

Unfortunately, William behaved badly at his nursery school, too. William was the first heir to the throne to attend preschool. Diana and Charles hoped William's behavior would improve if he was around other children. They sent him to Mrs. Mynor's Nursery School in Notting Hill Gate. They felt certain that children would not treat him like royalty. But things didn't change right away.

At first William was quite demanding around his schoolmates. He threatened to have them arrested if they would not play his way. There were some playground fights as well. It wasn't long before the prince had earned the nickname "Basher."

Prince Charles was very concerned about William's behavior. He knew that before long the newspapers would be writing about Will being

WILL IS THE
FIRST PAGE
BOY FOLLOW-
ING PRINCE
ANDREW, HIS
UNCLE, AND
SARAH
FERGUSON
DURING THEIR
WEDDING.

naughty. The worst was at the 1986 wedding of Charles's brother, Prince Andrew, to Sarah Ferguson.

Prince William was a page boy in the wedding party. The other children taking part in the ceremony were well behaved. But William stood out for all the wrong reasons. He refused to remain still while the couple exchanged vows. William also stuck out his tongue at the flower girls and bridesmaids.

After that, there were some changes at Kensington Palace. Nanny Barnes had always pampered William. Now, however, it was believed that a firmer hand was needed. Ruth Wallace became the new nanny.

Miss Wallace worked on discipline and manners with both William and Harry. She stressed the importance of being well behaved and polite. The change in William was noted within months. He learned to say "please" and "thank you." He also stopped being so bossy with classmates and servants.

The turnaround came just in time. William had completed nursery school. Now he would be with older children at Wetherby, a school known for its well-mannered pupils. Fortunately, Wetherby was

IN 1991, CHARLES AND DIANA HAD TO ATTEND THE OPENING OF
PARLIAMENT, BUT IT WAS CLEAR THEY WERE NOT HAPPY TOGETHER.

just fine for William. He got along with the other
boys and fit in well.

The family spent most weekends at Highgrove,
their country home in Gloucestershire. Both William
and his brother loved the nearly 350 acres (140
hectares) of farmland. At Highgrove the boys
climbed trees and rode horses.

Still, life was far from perfect. Through the years his parents had grown apart. Even their love for William and his brother could not keep their marriage together.

It would later become publicly known that Charles was seeing another woman. She was Camilla Parker Bowles. Charles had dated Camilla before his marriage.

Also, Diana was suffering from a sickness known as bulimia. She would eat large amounts of food and then force herself to throw up. Bulimics also exercise too much.

Charles and Diana began to spend more time apart. There was less and less family time for the boys to enjoy. Charles moved most of his clothes and things out of Kensington Palace to Highgrove.

Charles wanted to remain close to William. It was clear that he loved both boys. But the overall effect of the split between William's parents was becoming clear. This future king of Britain would not grow up in a happy home with both his parents. There would not be wonderful family outings. William would have to take what he could from each parent separately.

PRINCE
CHARLES HAS
ALWAYS
LOVED RID-
ING, AND HE
WAS GLAD TO
FIND THAT
HIS SONS
LOVED IT AS
WELL.

A TRIP TO
NIAGARA
FALLS

CHAPTER 4

Growing Up

Diana did not want William to miss out on any-
thing. She longed for him to be like other boys and
dreamed of a normal, carefree childhood for both
her sons. The Princess of Wales felt that her hus-
band's royal upbringing had isolated him from the
real world in many ways. Diana was determined that
things would be different for William.

Therefore, she planned wonderful outings for
William and Harry. Together the three rode go-
carts or enjoyed wild water rides at amusement

parks. Fancy palace dinners were balanced by trips to the movies and burgers and fries. When William was with Diana, he was allowed to dress like a kid. The British prince wore jeans, sweatshirts, and baseball caps.

William proved to be quite athletic. He became good at rugby, a popular game in Britain. To his father's delight he was also an excellent marksman. He had begun riding at a very young age and showed promise there too.

By the fall of 1990, William would have an important break from the day-to-day tensions of his home life. He had turned eight, and like other well-bred British boys, he was headed for boarding school.

His parents had decided on Ludgrove Preparatory School in Berkshire. There he shared a room with four other boys. The school was a good choice. It had a warm atmosphere and an excellent athletic program.

But there was another reason for picking it. Ludgrove was situated off a main road on 130 acres (53 hectares) of land. With any luck, Prince William would be shielded from the flashing cameras of photographers.

DIANA AND
WILL, ON A DAY
OFF FROM
LUDGROVE.

William did well at Ludgrove. During his five years there, he was on the school soccer, basketball, and swim teams. He was captain of Ludgrove's hockey and rugby teams as well. Although the press sometimes reported otherwise, William also did well in his school subjects.

During visits home, William saw how bad things were between his parents. On more than one occasion, he witnessed screaming battles between his mother and father.

William did his best to comfort Diana. After an unsettling argument, William came to his mother's aid. He phoned her favorite restaurant and made dinner reservations for the two of them.

The bond between mother and son tightened over time. Diana remained very involved in her son's life. She usually insisted on having the final say in decisions affecting the boy. This was evident when, in June 1991, William had a sports accident.

William had been playing golf with some boys at school when he was accidentally hit in the head with a golf club. Unfortunately, the injury was serious. After falling to the ground unconscious, William was rushed to the hospital.

Both Diana and Charles arrived shortly afterward. However, they argued over which medical center William would be taken to for the surgery he needed. In the end Diana won. She rode in the ambulance with William. Charles followed closely behind in his car. After the boy's operation for a skull fracture, Diana remained with William in his hospital room.

William loved his father. Yet he had become protective of Diana. He once told her that when he grew up he wanted to be a policeman so he could look out for her. However, his younger brother quickly pointed out that William couldn't be a policeman. He had to be king!

Prince William called Diana from school most nights. He also wrote to her regularly. Diana referred to William as "the man in my life." However, there were those who felt Diana relied too much on a ten-year-old boy.

DIANA SOMETIMES FOUND IT DIFFICULT TO APPEAR HAPPY IN PUBLIC WHEN HER MARRIAGE TO CHARLES WAS FALLING APART.

In the fall of 1992, the royal couple's marriage became headline news. Stories about their unhappiness filled the newspapers. The gossip was everywhere—even at Will's school.

Prince William could not see a newspaper or have a day go by without hearing something about his parents' squabbles. Later on, William would admit that every time he saw a picture of his mother or father on a front page, his heart sank. He knew it meant more embarrassing rumors to contend with.

In December 1992, Britain's Prime Minister, John Major, publicly announced that the royal couple was separating. Diana had driven up to Ludgrove the day before the announcement. She wanted her son to hear the news from her. Despite how he might have felt, William tried to put his mother first. He responded with the dignity of a true prince. William kissed his mother's cheek and said, "I hope you both will be happier now."

CHAPTER FIVE

New Times, New Challenges

The Christmas season was difficult for William that year. He tried not to show it, but he was embarrassed by his parents' very public parting. Friends said that William seemed more withdrawn. In the months ahead, his grades would drop as well.

Things improved with time, however. William did his best to adjust to his family's new situation. He and his brother continued to see their father at Highgrove. Of course, now their mother no longer went there with them.

Diana enjoyed a variety of sports with William. The two sometimes played tennis at Diana's health club. Both were also excellent swimmers. They frequently raced each other across the pool. William swam so well that his mother called him a fish.

The time William spent with his father tended to be more formal. Charles often reminded William about the importance of proper behavior and manners. Yet William greatly looked forward to riding, hunting, and fishing with Charles. These were some of the happiest times they spent together.

By the spring of 1993, visits to Highgrove became even better. This was due to the addition of a young woman named Alexandra "Tiggy" Legge-Bourke to Charles's staff. Tiggy acted as a nanny for the boys when they were at their father's. She also accompanied William and Harry on extended holiday visits to any of their grandmother's royal residences.

Tiggy was fun-loving and athletic. That was a combination both boys found hard to resist. William, Harry, and Tiggy climbed trees, ran races, rode horses, and swam together. Tiggy was an excellent shot, and she hunted with the boys. In their quieter moments, the three listened to music and watched videos.

As time passed, William became even more close to Tiggy. She was warm and friendly, yet had a good head on her shoulders. The young Prince felt that he could trust her. Being young herself, Tiggy seemed best able to understand William's feelings. He frequently asked her advice on many things.

Highgrove was now a much nicer place to visit. William did not miss the fights between his mother and father. Tiggy ate with the boys and Charles, and dinners were much more pleasant.

When his younger brother Harry was old enough to go to school at Ludgrove, William welcomed him. The boys liked being together and grew extremely close at school. William had always been protective of Diana. Now he was also protective of his brother.

William's final year at Ludgrove was probably his best. He did especially well in his school work and excelled on the soccer team. William had enjoyed Ludgrove's casual atmosphere, and the chance to be shielded from the press.

WILL ON
HIS FIRST
DAY AT ETON

In 1995, when William was thirteen, it was time for him to move on. He entered Eton, an excellent school that was extremely challenging. There he lived in an ivy-covered dorm known as the Manor House. Fifty other students resided there as well.

Each boy had his own room. William's was above the kitchen. Half the students had their own computers, but surprisingly, William wasn't one of them. He was the only student to have his own bathroom. Nevertheless, there were few other hints of special treatment.

William was generally expected to follow the same rules as the other boys. That meant no posters on his bedroom walls. He was permitted pinups on the inside of his locker door. At various times these included pictures of actress Pamela Anderson, models Cindy Crawford and Claudia Schiffer, and rock singer Baby Spice.

At school William wore the same uniform as the other Eton students. This consisted of striped pants and a black tailcoat. The initials "W.O.W." were on his school track outfit and swimsuit. That stood for William of Wales.

William was well liked and a good student at Eton. His best subjects were geography, biology, and art history. His artistic talent was also noticed. Some of William's artwork was chosen for a school exhibition. The prince received other honors at Eton as well. As a member of the school's cadet force, he won the Sword of Honor. This award is given to the student who is the most successful soldier of the year.

In addition, William was extremely active in school sports. He was captain of Eton's swim team and also played football, rugby, and water polo.

The prince's friends at Eton described him as being considerate yet "extremely laid back." William was known to enjoy computer games, action movies, techno music, dancing, and dressing casually. In most ways William was like the other upper-class, wealthy young men at Eton.

Of course, he was the only one who visited Windsor Castle on Sunday afternoons. That was where he had tea with his grandmother, the queen of Britain. At those times, his grandmother spoke to William about what would one day be expected of him as king. It was a look into the future for the student prince.

CHAPTER 6

It Shouldn't Have Happened

At Eton, William's dislike of press photographers became obvious. William had long hated the way photographers hounded his mother. He had often seen her come home in tears after being chased by them. The press had agreed not to photograph William and Harry at school. But photographers still frequently appeared during family outings and vacations.

Over time William developed ways to thwart them. He would refuse to smile and walked with his head down—a trick his mother was known to use. At large public events, William's friends helped. The

HERE, DIANA IS MEETING STEVEN SPIELBERG, THE DIRECTOR OF MANY FAMOUS MOVIES. AS USUAL, THE PHOTOGRAPHERS WERE MORE INTERESTED IN GETTING A PICTURE OF DIANA THAN OF THE OTHER CELEBRITIES AT THE EVENT.

boys he was with would surround him. That made it hard to tell William from the others.

When his parents finally divorced in 1996, Diana had first spoken to William about it. Despite his youth, the princess valued her son's opinion. His mother called William the perfect Gemini—serious yet sensitive.

But Diana still greatly influenced William too. She especially wanted William to know that his life did not have to be limited by tradition. Through her example, the prince saw that royals could directly reach out to help the poor, AIDS patients, landmine victims, and other people in trouble.

Diana made a point of sometimes taking her sons with her when doing charity work. It was important to William's mother that he meet people from different social backgrounds. Her efforts obviously made an impression. It was William who suggested that Diana auction off some of her evening gowns and dresses for charity.

Prince William also benefited from being with his father. As a young teenager, William found that he especially looked forward to the days he and his father went hunting. These outings were not always appreciated by animal-rights supporters though. In November 1996, a hunting incident involving Prince William and his father particularly upset them.

The problem arose after William shot his first deer. The prince killed the animal with a single bullet, making his father and others in their hunting party quite proud. As was customary, shortly afterward, William was "blooded." That entailed having the deer's blood smeared on his forehead. It was a ritual his father had gone through when he killed his first deer.

Britain's animal rights supporters were shocked and upset. They strongly criticized Charles for encouraging William to pursue this sport. The father and son listened but did not change their minds. The deer head was mounted and hung in Balmoral Castle. Charles and William continue to enjoy hunting together.

William would need a close relationship with his father when he was forced to go through the worst tragedy of his life. On August 31, 1997, his mother, Princess Diana, was killed in a car accident in France. That evening she had been riding in a car with her friend, Dodi Fayed, when they were chased by a group of press photographers. In an effort to lose them, the couple's driver had stepped on the gas, and a fatal accident happened. Except for the princess's bodyguard, everyone in the car was killed.

Though Charles and Diana had been divorced, Charles brought her body home from France. He also changed the formalities usually involved in royal funerals. Charles felt that Diana should have a funeral that reflected her lifestyle. That meant that

WILL AND HARRY
WALK BEHIND
THE CASKET WITH
THEIR GRAND-
FATHER, PRINCE
PHILIP; DIANA'S
BROTHER, EARL
SPENCER; AND
THEIR FATHER,
PRINCE CHARLES.

people from her favorite charities would be invited rather than mainly foreign heads of state. William was grateful for that and admired how Charles handled things.

Some say that after his mother's death, Prince William grew up overnight. He had long been protective of Harry, but now he doubled his efforts. In the days after Diana died, the brothers took long walks together. William tried to comfort Harry whenever possible.

Both boys would need one another on the day of their mother's funeral. William and Harry joined their father, grandfather, and uncle (Diana's brother) in the mile-long walk to Westminster Abbey for the funeral service. The five silently walked behind the gun carriage carrying the princess's coffin. They passed streets lined with thousands of mourners. The air was heavy with grief, but the only sound was the quiet sobbing coming from the crowd.

Diana's tragic death resulted in an outcry against photographers. William personally blamed the photographers for his mother's death. He knew that the car's driver had been drinking and had driven too fast. Still, he believed that his mother would be alive if she hadn't been chased for a picture.

CHAPTER 7

A Royal Young Adult

As William grew older, he began to draw quite a bit of attention. Many believed it was the combination of his good looks and quiet charm. People also could not resist comparing him to his mother. In any case, young girls adored the handsome prince. It soon became obvious that William was going to be a teenage heartthrob.

When going to the fiftieth wedding anniversary lunch of his grandparents (Queen Elizabeth II and Prince Phillip) in November 1997, William was greeted by a crowd of more than six hundred screaming girls.

They carried signs that read "I love you," or "I'm your princess." Along with his fans came a herd of tabloid photographers. After Diana's experience, William's dislike for press photographers had only deepened. Charles tried to help. He explained to his son that one way or another the press would always be in their lives. The teenage prince tried to accept that.

As a future king of Britain, William realizes that he will remain in the limelight. His eighteenth birthday, on June 21, 2000, was noted in newspapers in numerous countries. To honor him that day, the British island of Jersey issued a series of stamps with Prince William's picture.

The young royal has also come to accept that there are some things he cannot do. William never travels on an airplane with his father. That way, if there was a fatal accident, both direct heirs to the throne would not be lost.

When traveling, Charles and William's younger brother, Harry, fly in one plane. William flies in another. Other security measures include the detectives or bodyguards who follow William at all times. The prince wears an electronic tracking bracelet as well. This permits his location to be known wherever he is.

HAPPY 18TH BIRTHDAY, WILLIAM!

In 2000, William graduated from Eton. He was accepted at the University of St. Andrews in Scotland. The prince decided to take a year off before entering the university. This is not uncommon in Britain. The time off is known as a "gap year."

During that time William traveled and became involved in some educational and service projects. His first trip was to a jungle in Belize. There he participated in military exercises with the Welsh Guard, a part of the British army. The prince also took part in a three-week marine-conservation program on Rodrigues Island in the Indian Ocean. In early October 2000, William headed for a base camp in the mountains of Chile. There the prince helped with various environmental projects. Extra time was set aside for some adventure travel too.

William is rumored to have dated a number of young women. But this prince does not kiss and tell. William has said that he likes to keep his private life private. So far he has. Nevertheless, he has denied rumors that he ever dated pop singer Britney Spears.

Like many young men, William likes fast cars. He is said to have enjoyed speeding around the back roads of Balmoral. For his seventeenth birthday, his father bought him his first car. It was a Volkswagen Golf. On his eighteenth birthday he received a Kawasaki motorcycle.

Prince William has developed a great sense of style. *People* magazine even named the young prince to its best-dressed list. One summer William wore a trendy pair of Killer Loop sunglasses to a polo

PRINCE
WILLIAM'S
TRIP TO
CHILE WAS
PHYSICALLY
CHALLENGING
BUT FUN.

match. Afterward, London's Oxford Street Sunglass Hut was mobbed with young people wanting to buy them.

When not at school, William spends much of his time at Highgrove. But as his mother did, he enjoys London's night life. So sometimes he stays at St. James's Palace—his father's London residence. William has his own top-floor suite there.

Because he is a prince, much of William's life is already planned out. Undoubtedly though, William has a mind of his own. Some call it a stubborn streak. Others, more politely, refer to him as a determined young man. Either way, the British press has already dubbed him "Willful Will."

Usually at eighteen, someone in William's position is called "Your Royal Highness." William has passed on that. For the time being, he still wants to be called just "William." This is partly because he will not be taking on royal duties while at the University of St. Andrews. He has also decided against hiring a personal secretary to keep track of his engagements and mail.

Royal watchers wonder whether this future king will want to change the monarchy. William has already questioned why so many palaces are necessary.

To many people, William's promise seems limitless. He is often described as having his mother's way with people and his father's intellect. No one knows what path he will choose after graduating from St. Andrews. He is second in line for the throne, after his father. William has been described as a king-in-waiting.

One day he will be King William V. Some say he will create a new beginning for Britain's royalty. His grandmother, Queen Elizabeth II, has high hopes for him. She has privately predicted that William will bring the monarchy into the twenty-first century. But that's a story yet to be told.

BRITAIN'S FUTURE KING

IMPORTANT DATES

June 21, 1982	Prince William is born.
March 1983	William accompanies his parents on a trip to Australia and New Zealand.
September 15, 1984	William's brother, Harry, is born.
September 1985	William enters Mrs. Mynor's Nursery School.
September 1990	William goes off to Ludgrove Preparatory, a boarding school.
June 1991	William is accidentally struck on the head with a golf club. Surgery is required.
December 1992	William's parents separate.
Spring 1993	Tiggy Legge-Bourke is hired as a companion for William and Harry.
September 1995	William enters Eton.
August 1996	Diana and Charles divorce.
June 1997	At William's suggestion, Diana auctions off some of her gowns and dresses for charity.
August 31, 1997	Diana is killed in an automobile accident.
September 6, 1997	William attends his mother's funeral.
June 21, 1999	William turns seventeen. He is given his first car as a birthday gift.
June 21, 2000	William turns eighteen. Having graduated from Eton, William takes a year off before beginning at the university.
September 2001	William enters the University of St. Andrews.

FURTHER READING

BOOKS ABOUT PRINCE WILLIAM

Degnen, Lisa. *Prince William: Prince of Hearts*. New York: Warner Books, 1998.

Murphy, Catherine. *Prince William*. Kansas City: Andrews McMeel Publishing, 1998.

Rand, Gloria. *Prince William*. New York: Henry Holt, 1994.

BOOKS ABOUT ROYALS

Krohn, Katherine E. *Princess Diana*. Minneapolis: Lerner, 1999.

Somerset, Fry-Plantagenet. *Kings and Queens of England and Scotland*. New York: Dorling Kindersley, 1999.

Stone, Tanya Lee. *Diana: Princess of the People*. Brookfield, CT.: The Millbrook Press, 1999.

Wood, Richard. *Diana: The People's Princess*. Austin, TX: Raintree Steck Vaughn, 1998.

BOOKS ABOUT BRITAIN

Flint, David. *The United Kingdom*. Austin, TX: Raintree Steck Vaughn, 1994.

Langley, Andrew. *Passport to Britain*. Danbury, CT: Franklin Watts, 1994.

INDEX

Page numbers in **bold** refer to illustrations.

Anderson, Mabel, 9
Anderson, Pamela, 31
Andrew, Prince, **16**, 17

Barnes, Barbara, 9, 17
Belize, 42
Bowles, Camilla Parker, 19

Charles, Prince of Wales,
    5, **7**, **8**, 9–12, **10**, 14,
    15, **18**, 19, 22, 24–29,
    35, 36, **37**, 38, 40, 45
Chile, 42, **43**
Crawford, Cindy, 31

Diana, Princess of Wales,
    8, **25**, 27, **34**, 44, 45
    baptism of William, 6, **7**
    death of, 36, **37**, 38
    divorce of, 4, 19, 26,
        27, 34
    marriage to Charles, 5,
        18, 19, 24–26
    as mother, 8–12, 14, **20**,
        21–22, **23**, 24–25,
        28
    press and, 33, 38
    relationship with
        William, 9, 10,
        24–26, 29, 34–35

Elizabeth, the Queen
    Mother, 6, **7**

Elizabeth II, Queen, 5, **7**,
    10, 10, 14, 32, 39, 45
Eton, **30**, 31–32

Fayed, Dodi, 36

Harry, Prince, 12–13, **13**,
    17–19, **20**, 25, 28, 29,
    37, 38
Highgrove, 18, 27, 29, 44

Legge-Bourke, Alexandra
    "Tiggy," 28–29
Ludgrove Preparatory
    School, 22, 24, 26

Major, John, 26

People magazine, 42
Philip, Prince, **7**, **37**, 38, 39

Rodrigues Island, 42

Sarah, Duchess of York, **16**,
    17
Schiffer, Claudia, 31
Spears, Britney, 42
Spencer, Earl, **37**, 38
Spice, Baby, 31
Spielberg, Steven, 34

University of St. Andrews,
    41, 44

Wallace, Ruth, 17
Welsh Guard, 42

William, Prince of Wales,
    3, **45**
    artistic talent of, 32
    baptism of, 6, **7**
    birth of, 5, 6
    childhood of, **8**, 8–15,
        15, **16**, 17–18, **20**,
        21–22, **23**, 24–29
    death of mother and, 4,
        36, **37**, 38
    divorce of parents and,
        4, 19, 26, 27, 34
    education of, 14, 17–18,
        22, 24, 29, **30**, 31–32
    eighteenth birthday of,
        40, **41**
    "gap year" and, 41–42,
        43
    hunting and, 35–36
    nicknames of, 11, 15
    physical appearance of,
        4
    press and, 22, 33–34,
        38, 40
    private life of, 42
    relationship with
        brother, 13, 29, 38
    relationship with
        mother, 9, 10,
        24–26, 29, 34–35
    relationship with
        "Tiggy," 28–29
    security measures and,
        40
    sports and, 22, 24, 28,
        29, 32